CELTIC
GODS, HEROES, AND MYTHOLOGY

BY JUNE SMALLS

CONTENT CONSULTANT
Glen Robert Gill
Associate Professor, Classics and General Humanities
Montclair State University

Cover image: Arthur is one of the most famous heroes of Celtic mythology.

Core Library

An Imprint of Abdo Publishing
abdobooks.com

abdocorelibrary.com

Published by Abdo Publishing, a division of ABDO, PO Box 398166, Minneapolis, Minnesota 55439. Copyright © 2019 by Abdo Consulting Group, Inc. International copyrights reserved in all countries. No part of this book may be reproduced in any form without written permission from the publisher. Core Library™ is a trademark and logo of Abdo Publishing.

Printed in the United States of America, North Mankato, Minnesota
092018
012019

THIS BOOK CONTAINS RECYCLED MATERIALS

Cover Photo: GraphicaArtis/Hulton Archive/Getty Images
Interior Photos: GraphicaArtis/Hulton Archive/Getty Images, 1; Historica Graphica Collection Heritage Images/Newscom, 4–5; Gigi Peis/Shutterstock Images, 8, 45; Geography Photos/ Universal Images Group/Getty Images, 10; Werner Forman/Universal Images Group/Getty Images, 12–13, 23 (top), 33, 43; Artur Widak/NurPhoto/Getty Images, 14; Florilegius/Alamy, 17; Uladzimir Zgurski/Shutterstock Images, 18; Stephen Barnes/Shutterstock Images, 20–21; Shutterstock Images, 23 (bottom left), 23 (bottom right), 24; DeAgostini/Getty Images, 28–29; iStockphoto, 36–37; Mike Kemp/In Pictures/Getty Images, 39

Editor: Marie Pearson
Series Designer: Ryan Gale

Library of Congress Control Number: 2018949781

Publisher's Cataloging-in-Publication Data

Names: Smalls, June, author.
Title: Celtic gods, heroes, and mythology / by June Smalls.
Description: Minneapolis, Minnesota : Abdo Publishing, 2019 | Series: Gods, heroes, and mythology | Includes online resources and index.
Identifiers: ISBN 9781532117794 (lib. bdg.) | ISBN 9781532170652 (ebook)
Subjects: LCSH: Celtic mythology--Juvenile literature. | Celtic gods--Juvenile literature. | Heroes--Juvenile literature.
Classification: DDC 299.16--dc23

CONTENTS

GIANT'S CAUSEWAY

Fionn MacCumhaill, also known as Finn MacCool, is probably the most famous hero of Irish legend. Tales of this gentle giant and great warrior leader are told in Scotland, too. Finn studied under the tutor Finnegas. Finnegas had spent years fishing for the Salmon of Knowledge. This fish could give a person all the knowledge in the world. At last, Finnegas caught the mythical creature. He gave it to Finn to cook. Finn burned his thumb on the hot fish. When he put his thumb in his mouth to soothe the burn, he accidentally tasted some of the fish and gained wisdom. After that, whenever he had a problem, Finn

Finn, *right*, was married to Oonagh.

KING ARTHUR

The story of King Arthur has its roots in Celtic mythology. It may have originated in Wales or northern Britain. Arthur may have been based on a real-life figure. But his story changed over time as it was retold again and again. Some early stories present him as a hero of war. Later stories show him as a great king. Christians also retold the Arthur legend, adding new details, so it is hard to know for certain the original tale of Arthur.

would stick his thumb in his mouth in order to know the answers.

Finn was a giant, but he was not a very big one. Another giant, Benandonner, lived across the sea from him. The two giants shouted boasts and threats at one another. Each challenged the other to prove who was stronger. But no ship could carry the heavy giants. At last, Finn threw rocks into the water to create a bridge so they could meet in battle. After creating the bridge, Finn was worn out from the work. He fell fast asleep.

Oonagh, Finn's wife, heard Benandonner approaching. She saw that he was much larger than Finn and knew he would beat Finn in a fight. Thinking quickly, she covered the sleeping Finn in a blanket and put a bonnet on his head.

The giant arrived and demanded to know where Finn was. Oonagh shushed him. She told him he could wait for Finn, but he had to be quiet so he would not wake the baby. Benandonner, not realizing the baby was Finn in disguise, panicked. If Finn's baby was that big, then Finn must be enormous! He ran away in fear. His retreat destroyed the bridge, creating a jumble of rocks in the water. Today, this rock formation can still be seen along the coastline of Northern Ireland. It is known as the Giant's Causeway. It is a favorite spot for tourists.

CELTIC HISTORY

The Celts were a people who lived in western Europe from 500 BCE to 500 CE. They were not just a single people or class. They were groups of people connected

The unique shape of the stones at Giant's Causeway make this site a popular place to visit.

by language and culture. Each group had its own leaders. They never created a central government.

The Celts shared their stories and history orally through the songs and poems of the bards and druids. The bards were musicians and poets. The druids were wise people who served as priests, teachers, and judges.

Continental Celts were those who lived on the European continent. Insular Celts lived in the

British Isles. In approximately 100 CE, Romans conquered the continent. There, the tales of Celtic gods and creatures faded. Only what the Romans recorded is left to be studied today. However, the Celts who settled in the British Isles held on to their stories. Here, Celtic myths and legends survived.

Myths and legends are stories that are important to a culture. Myths often involve gods, magical beings, and supernatural events. Legends are stories about famous events or people. Myths and legends can tell truths that more realistic-sounding stories cannot.

BARDS AND DRUIDS

Celtic history was originally shared orally rather than being written down. Bards wrote and recited stories. The epic stories usually showed heroes and their journeys or deeds. Druids were educated Celts. In addition to studying ancient lore, they also studied natural philosophy and astronomy. According to the Romans, who wrote about their encounters with the Celts, druids spent up to 20 years training.

Because their history and legends were shared orally at first, there are multiple versions of most Celtic stories. Later, these stories were written down, especially in Ireland. Some myths and gods are only linked to certain villages or clans. Some gods are known by more than one name. Some of the Celtic stories changed over the years with retellings. It is likely that some stories were based on real people and events. The well-known tale of King Arthur is one possible example.

EXPLORE ONLINE

A sidebar in Chapter One talks about the story of King Arthur. The article at the website below gives additional information on King Arthur. Does the article answer any of the questions you had about King Arthur? Do you believe King Arthur is based on a real man from history?

BBC: ARTHUR
abdocorelibrary.com/celtic-mythology

Artifacts found at ancient Celtic village sites have given researchers clues about what the Celts believed.

GODS AND GODDESSES

Celtic mythology is full of tales of gods and goddesses. Some Celtic groups had different names for the same god. Some gods were specific to small villages on the continent or in the isles.

These gods had powers. They could directly affect the natural world. If people wanted help from a god or deity, they would make an offering. To appeal to a water god, for example, people may have thrown a jewel, weapons, or other valuable items into a well, lake, or river.

Cernunnos is one of many Celtic gods.

People in Ireland still incorporate images of Dagda in their celebrations today.

WHO WERE THESE GODS?

Dagda was the god of life and death. He was known as a good god and as father of the gods. He had all the wisdom and could handle any task. Dagda had three daughters. Each was named Brigid. One was the goddess of wisdom, magic, and poetry. The second was the goddess of healing and fertility. The third protected metalworkers and other craftspeople.

Danu was called the Mother Goddess. She created the Tuatha Dé Danann. The Tuatha were a race of gods with great magical abilities. After Celts began adopting Christianity, they started seeing the Tuatha as fairies instead of gods. One of these Tuatha was Lugh. His name means "the Shining One." He was skilled as a blacksmith, musician, warrior, poet, and scholar. He is the most well-known hero of the Tuatha. Continental Celts called him Lugus.

Dian Cécht was the god of medicine. Water from his magical springs could heal dead or wounded warriors. He created

CAULDRONS

Cauldrons show up many times in Celtic mythology. Dagda's cauldron never ran empty of food. The Cauldron of Knowledge held a potion that granted wisdom. The potion had to cook for a year and a day. The Cauldron of Bran the Blessed could heal injured warriors placed inside it.

an arm out of silver for King Nuada, who lost his arm in battle, becoming unfit to serve as king. A man named

SHAPE-SHIFTERS

There are many stories of shape-shifters in Celtic mythology. Stories tell of humans transforming into animals such as wolves, pigs, deer, or butterflies. There are also creatures that can take human form. These include the kelpies and the selkies.

Bres took the throne. After Nuada received his new arm, he fought Bres to regain his place as king. On the day of the battle, Lugh helped Nuada in every way. He helped with weapons. He led troops. He cast spells along with druids. Finally, Nuada won the battle. Years later, the Celts would battle and defeat the Tuatha. The Tuatha moved to the sídh, or fairy mounds.

GODS OF NATURE

On the continent and occasionally on the British Isles, one well-known god was Cernunnos. He was the god of animals, the hunt, and fertility. His name means "Horned One." He had the antlers of a stag.

Irish tradition taught that Lugh, *right*, was a triplet, but his two brothers died.

THE ANCIENT IRISH
ALPHABET

The ancient Irish alphabet, called ogham for the god credited with creating it, had 25 symbols. The alphabet can be seen carved into wood or standing stones. It is nicknamed the "Celtic Alphabet Tree" because most of the symbols are named after trees. Inscriptions in ogham are read from the bottom to the top, just like climbing a tree. There are some that read from left to right. Why do you think a language written vertically would be useful for writing on standing stones?

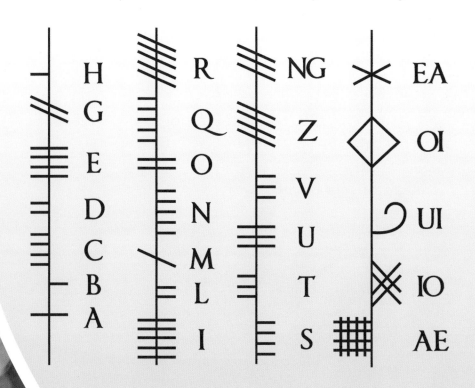

Manannan was god of the sea. This god was a great magician. He made a golden cup that shattered if someone lied. He made a silver branch with three golden apples. The apples made music and had healing powers. Manannan had a boat that sailed itself. He rode atop the seas in a horse-drawn chariot.

Morrigan was a shape-shifting goddess of battle. She could turn into a raven. She also foretold who would die in battle.

Ogma, or Oghma, was the god of eloquence. He spoke so sweetly that those who listened became enchanted. He is said to have invented the ancient Irish alphabet.

NATURE, SPIRITS, AND CREATURES

The Celts believed all natural things had spirits. From bodies of water to trees to animals, all were considered important and were honored. Trees, especially the oak tree, were sacred. Celts also believed the spiritual world and the natural world were connected. So people worshipped outside in gatherings led by the druids. Groves of trees were a favorite gathering place. There, people could be close to the mythical creatures and gods that were connected to certain places or natural features.

Druids held many ceremonies near oak trees.

CREATURES

In Celtic mythology, the world was full of many magical creatures. Just like the gods, some were widely known while others were specific to a place or group. For example, the banshee was a common figure in Irish lore. This female spirit had a horrible wail that foretold a family member's death. Some said she was a young maiden. Others described her as an old crone.

Giants appeared in both continental and insular mythology. Some giants in these stories were just like ordinary men, only larger and stronger. Other giants, such as Balor, chief of the Fomorians, had powers.

SYMBOLS IN
CELTIC ART

There are a variety of symbols used in Celtic art. One is the Celtic knot. In Celtic mythology, knots stand for the interconnectedness of the universe. Some knots appear endless, with no beginning or end. The Celtic Tree of Life shows the roots and branches intertwining in the form of a knot. Knots and other symbols decorated warriors' shields. A famous example is the Battersea shield. The number three also had important meaning to Celts. The triple spiral is a Celtic symbol found on a number of ancient sites and tombs.

BATTERSEA SHIELD

TREE OF LIFE

TRIPLE SPIRAL

The modern Welsh flag with a red dragon has been used since 1959.

Balor was from insular stories. He had a huge poisonous eye. It could kill anything it gazed upon.

Welsh dragons were sometimes wingless water serpents. Other times they had the wings of a bat. Dragons were creatures of magic. They could affect how magic flowed through the land. Dragons connected the earth and sky. They guarded gates to other worlds. After Christianity arrived, dragons were often shown as evil. But today, a dragon is on the Welsh flag.

Celts on the islands told of the selkie. This gentle shape-shifting creature came from insular mythology. The selkie looked like a seal, but it could remove its sealskin and walk the earth as a human. Later, the selkie could put its skin back on to return to the sea. However, if the selkie ever lost its skin, it would be trapped as a human forever.

In Scotland, the kelpie was a shape-shifting water spirit. Sometimes it would take the form of a horse and lure humans to ride it. Then it would take the rider on a dangerous gallop. The rider could not dismount. The kelpie would carry the rider into the water and eat him or her. Kelpies could also shift into human form. But kelpies had a weakness. If someone got hold of one's bridle, that person would have command over the kelpie.

ANIMAL HELPERS

Animals are shown in Celtic jewelry, tapestries, clothing, and artwork. They represent important strengths or traits. For example, the boar can be a symbol of war and hunting or of feasting and kindness. The owl symbolizes wisdom and patience. Owls were believed to be guides in the Otherworld, which was the Celtic spirit world or afterlife.

The Celts believed people should have a close connection with animals and nature. Druids sometimes traveled to the Otherworld to interact

ANIMAL SYMBOLISM

Different animals represent different things in Celtic mythology. The deer represents the hunt, woodland, change, and the Otherworld. The dog stands for protection and shape-shifting. The dragon is for earth, magic, and the power of the land. The horse represents the sun, mystery, and creation. The raven stands for death, war, and healing. And the salmon is for knowledge, mystery, and emotion.

with animals. If druids needed help with a specific problem, they would call on certain animals. If they needed healing, animals such as the raven or snake were called. Bears, cats, dogs, and geese were called for protection.

Sometimes a special bond formed between a person and an individual animal. If the bond was strong enough, then that animal became a spiritual companion. Animals helped teach and guide people and even came to people in their dreams. They became partners on a person's life journey.

FURTHER EVIDENCE

Chapter Three discusses animals in Celtic mythology. What was one of the main points of this chapter? What evidence is included to support this point? Read the article at the website below. Does the information on the website support the main point of the chapter? Does it present new evidence?

DRUID ANIMAL LORE

abdocorelibrary.com/celtic-mythology

BEGINNINGS, WARS, AND THE OTHERWORLD

Celts had many stories telling how gods, goddesses, and creatures interacted with one another and with the human world. Few stories remain intact today. Most stories from continental Celtic mythology have been pieced together based on art and artifacts.

One continental Celtic story tells of the mare Eiocha. She had several children, including the god Cernunnos. Eiocha's children were lonely. They used the wood from an oak

The Gundestrup Cauldron gives historians clues about Celtic mythology.

tree to create the first man and woman. Cernunnos also made animals from the wood. He then commanded the oak to spread and grow. It created a forest for his animals to live in.

Eiocha's other children also created parts of the world. Epona created the horse in memory of her mother. Teutates created a bow, arrows, and a club. Taranis created thunderbolts. They could split the earth with fire and noise. Maponos created a harp. The wind and birds joined

QUESTS AND HEROES

Many Celtic myths tell of a hero on a quest. Quests include hunting, sailing across the seas, or searching for treasures such as magical cauldrons. These stories taught the values of strength, honor, and love in the face of loss. Heroes were gifted with sharp minds and physical strength. But they were not perfect. Sometimes they got angry. Sometimes they didn't listen to warnings and were punished with a curse. They were sometimes foolish or afraid. But the great heroes were always brave and did the right thing in the end.

him in music. Animals came from all around to hear him play.

The giants of the sea became jealous and attacked the gods. The gods fought and pushed them back into the sea. Epona rescued one man and one woman from the battle. These were the first of the mighty Celtic people.

THE OTHERWORLD

Celts believed that when people died, their souls went to the Otherworld. The living could also enter the Otherworld. It was seen as a peaceful place that coexisted with the world of the living. Heroes of the past, such as Arthur, waited there until they were needed again.

The Otherworld was sometimes known as the home of the Tuatha Dé Danann, or fairy folk. Some believed the Otherworld was under mounds in the ground called fairy mounds, typically hidden from human eyes. Others believed the Otherworld was located on islands west of Ireland or under the sea.

VOYAGE TO THE OTHERWORLD

One Irish story tells of Bran mac Febail's trip to the Otherworld. Bran was a giant in Welsh myth, but a human in Irish tradition. One day, Bran was hypnotized to sleep by music. When he woke, a woman sang to him about the joys of the sea. He gathered a crew and sailed, led by the music of Manannan, the god of the sea. They traveled to the islands of the Otherworld. One was the Isle of Women,

WHERE IS THE OTHERWORLD?

Many tales tell of heroes traveling to and from the Otherworld. In some stories, doors or gateways through caves or fairy mounds lead to the Otherworld. Other times travelers go by ship and reach islands in the Otherworld. On the Isle of Joy, people would experience happiness the moment they stepped on the island. Visitors to the Land of Youth could stay young and healthy forever.

Sailors may have offered model ships to Manannan for a safe voyage.

where no man lived. They stayed for one year before becoming homesick.

The chief woman warned Bran not to return home, but Bran did not listen. He sailed back to Ireland. As his ship neared the coast, he called to the people there, telling them he was Bran, son of Febail. He was returning home after a year of voyaging.

According to Irish tradition, the people answered that they knew no one by that name. But they knew his name from stories. They said once, long ago, a man named Bran had set out to sea and never returned. On hearing this, one of the seamen leapt from the ship to the beach. As soon as his feet touched the sand, he turned into ashes. The sailors realized to their horror that although they had been gone only one year in the Otherworld, many years had passed back home. The sailors now knew they could not return home. Bran called out his story to those on the beach. Then he turned his ship around. He and his crew are still sailing from island to island.

STRAIGHT TO THE
SOURCE

Jenny Butler teaches religious studies at University College Cork in Ireland. In a 2013 interview, she explained Celtic beliefs about the Otherworld:

> *In Celtic myth, in both Welsh and Irish mythologies, the otherworld is believed to be located either on an island or underneath the earth. In Irish, the otherworld is called Tír na nÓg or Land of Youth, also referred to as Tír Tairngire, Land of Promise. In this place, death and sickness do not exist. It was where the Tuatha Dé Danann, the "tribe of Anu," the mythical people associated with the fairies of later folklore, settled when they left Ireland's surface. Tír na nÓg is described as being underground or under the ocean and in folklore it is said to be accessible by certain special places on the landscape. These places include the fairy mounds or 'fairy forts.' Particular caves are also believed to be entrances to the otherworld.*

> Source: Emmett McIntyre. "Interview with Dr. Jenny Butler: The Celtic Folklore Traditions of Halloween." *Transceltic*, October 26, 2016. Web. Accessed June 19, 2018.

What's the Big Idea?
Take a close look at this passage. What different beliefs did the Celts have about the location of the Otherworld? Name two or three details that support this.

THEN AND NOW

Celtic culture has always been rich in music, art, and spirituality. People throughout Western Europe and the British Isles still celebrate Celtic culture. They make or buy jewelry and tattoos with complicated Celtic knots. Characters from the Irish alphabet, ogham, decorate jewelry and other items. People perform Celtic music with pipes, drums, and voices. Some people also practice the religion Druidism, which teaches harmony with nature.

Around the world, Celtic traditions and superstitions have left their mark. Kissing under the mistletoe, bonfires in the fall, and

Celtic knots are popular jewelry decorations.

throwing a coin into a well come from Celtic traditions. All Hallows' Eve was originally a Celtic festival called Samhain. Today, many call it Halloween. Celtic mythology was born long ago. But its stories have changed and adapted to new generations.

MISTLETOE

Mistletoe is a plant with many qualities in Celtic mythology. It heals, offers fertility, protects from witchcraft, and brings good luck. Druids would cut mistletoe from an oak on the winter solstice, the day with the shortest amount of daylight, and give it to people. This gift protected them from evil spirits.

DRUIDISM AND MYSTERIES

Some people practice Druidism today. It is an eco-religion. This means it emphasizes being in touch with the environment and the elements. Followers value knowledge, creativity, and living in tune with the natural world. Druids today are those

Modern druids hold ceremonies based on the cycles of the sun and moon.

STORYTELLING

Long ago, Celtic bards used music and poetry to share their tales. Storytelling taught people about their shared history and cultural values. Cultures all around the world have shared in this oral tradition, passing along their wisdom by word of mouth. Even today, families and close-knit groups of friends may have their own stories that they tell and retell.

who follow Druidism. They may work as healers. Or they may rescue animals. They may write and share art. A druid is always learning.

Even those who do not practice Druidism are fascinated with Celtic mythology. Tourists travel from all over the world to visit the Giant's Causeway in Northern Ireland. People fishing in the waters near the British Isles still wonder at the seals that play alongside their fishing boats. Are they actually selkies? Books and movies share Celtic tales. Still, sharing stories by word of mouth will always be a part of the Celtic tradition.

STRAIGHT TO THE
SOURCE

Ár nDraíocht Féin, or A Druid Fellowship, is a church that follows Celtic beliefs today. The church website describes some of the beliefs members share:

> *We believe that divinity is intrinsically present in the material and natural world, including in human nature. Divinity manifests as an uncountable number of beings, commonly called the Gods and Spirits. These can manifest at any point in space or time which They might choose, including within human beings. . . . We believe that it is necessary to have respect and love for Nature as divine in Her own right, and to accept ourselves as part of Nature and not Her "rulers." Many of us accept . . . that the biosphere of our planet is a living being, to who is due all the love and support that we, Her children, can give.*

> Source: Isaac Bonewits. "What Do Neopagan Druids Believe?" *ADF Basics.* Ár nDraíocht Féin: A Druid Fellowship, 2018. Web. Accessed June 19, 2018.

Point of View

The author of this passage is using evidence to support a point. Write a paragraph describing the point the author is making. Then write down two or three pieces of evidence the author uses to make the point.

FAST FACTS

Gods
- Dagda was the good god or father of the gods.

- Danu was the Mother Goddess who created the Tuatha Dé Danann.

- Dian Cécht was the god of medicine.

- Manannan was the god of the sea.

- Morrigan was the goddess of battle. She could shape-shift into many forms.

- Ogma was the god of eloquence. He created the ancient Irish alphabet.

Creatures
- Dragons represent power and wisdom. They guard gates to other worlds.

- Kelpies are water spirits that sometimes take the form of horses.

- Selkies are shape-shifting seals that can remove their skin to take on human form.

Stories
- One Celtic creation story tells how Eiocha's children created parts of the world.

- Many stories were told about the Celtic hero Finn MacCool. One tale explains how a fight between Finn and another giant created the rock formation known as the Giant's Causeway.

- A story of Bran mac Febail tells of Bran's voyage to the islands of the Otherworld.

STOP AND
THINK

You Are There

Chapter One talks about how Finn MacCool built Giant's Causeway. Imagine you are watching him build it and see Benandonner crossing it to fight Finn. Write a letter to a friend explaining what happened. Be sure to add plenty of detail to your notes.

Surprise Me

Chapter Three discusses Celtic mythological creatures. After reading this book, what two or three facts about mythological creatures did you find most surprising? Write a few sentences about each fact. Why did you find each fact surprising?

Say What?

Studying Celtic mythology can mean learning a lot of new vocabulary. Find five words in this book you've never heard before. Use a dictionary to find out what they mean. Then write the meanings in your own words, and use each word in a new sentence.

Why Do I Care?

You might not share Celtic beliefs. But that doesn't mean you can't think about the importance of world religions. How does religion affect your daily life? Write down two or three reasons why learning about different religious beliefs is important in today's world.

GLOSSARY

bard
a musician or poet who wrote and recited often-epic stories of heroes and their journeys or deeds

culture
the shared beliefs and practices of a group

deity
a god, goddess, or divine being

druid
an educated person in Celtic culture who acted as a priest, teacher, or judge

fertility
the ability to produce offspring or crops

mare
a female horse

oral tradition
the sharing of information or stories by word of mouth

quest
a long journey in search of something

supernatural
describing beings or events that do not follow the laws of nature

ONLINE
RESOURCES

To learn more about Celtic gods, heroes, and mythology, visit our free resource websites below.

Visit **abdocorelibrary.com** for free Common Core resources for teachers and students, including vetted activities, multimedia, and booklinks, for deeper subject comprehension.

Visit **abdobooklinks.com** for free additional online weblinks for further learning. These links are routinely monitored and updated to provide the most current information available.

LEARN
MORE

Randolph, Joanne. *Celtic Myths and Legends.* New York: Cavendish Square, 2018.

Star, Fleur, ed. *What Do You Believe?* New York: DK, 2016.

INDEX

About the Author

June Smalls loves mythical creatures. She lives in Virginia with her husband, daughter, and an assortment of odd animals. She never stops learning because there is always something new and amazing to discover.